GOOD THINGS

Happen Most of the Time,

BUT BAD THINGS

Happen...Sometimes

Kristy Scholar

ISBN 979-8-89428-828-4 (paperback)
ISBN 979-8-89428-829-1 (digital)

Christian Faith Publishing
832 Park Avenue
Meadville, PA 16335
www.christianfaithpublishing.com

Printed in the United States of America

In loving memory of
Bryan—loved and missed, all day, every day

1

Sometimes, no matter what, EVERYTHING seems to go our way. Nothing can go wrong. This makes us smile. We are happy and excited. What fun we are having!

But sometimes NOTHING goes our way, and everything seems to go wrong! This can make us feel very sad or even angry and confused.

Sometimes we get a puppy or a kitty who is frisky and very playful. This makes us so happy; we feel warm and fuzzy inside. We play with them as much as we can. We love them so much!

But sometimes our kitty or puppy can get very sick or just get old and die. This makes us very sad. We cry and miss them so much. We wonder why this had to happen.

Sometimes it seems that we are friends with everyone. This makes us so happy! We play, frolic, and have fun together.

But sometimes we aren't friends with everybody, and they tease us or make fun of us. This makes us sad, hurt, and confused. Why were we friends before, and now we're not?

Sometimes we can play all day without getting hurt. This makes us happy and daring. We can do anything!

But sometimes we do get hurt. This makes us cry. We are sad because we have to stop playing. *Why wasn't I more careful?* I wonder.

Sometimes we don't know that somebody, like a family member, friend, or somebody we know, can die. We are happy, and we feel safe with our family and friends. We think that they will be with us forever.

But sometimes a parent, grandparent, brother or sister, friend, or somebody we know does die. We are sad, confused, and even angry. We miss the person who died very much. Where are they? Why did this happen? Will I ever see them again?

Sometimes we are playing happily with our friends, and it is so much fun. We feel included and carefree! It's nice to have friends.

But sometimes we are left out, and it is not so much fun. It makes us feel so sad and confused. Why was I not included in the fun? What did I do to make this happen?

Sometimes you get to do something that you really want to do. This makes you excited and very happy. Things are going your way.

But sometimes you don't get your way and do something that you really wanted to do. This makes you angry and sad. *Why can't I do what I want to do*? you wonder.

We need to remember to appreciate the good times. We also need to remember that bad things happen sometimes. They will make us question, they will make us sad, angry, hurt, and confused, but we will feel better…sometime.

About the Author

Kristy was born in Michigan and moved to Minnesota as a young girl. She attended high school in Aurora, Minnesota, and obtained her degree in paralegal studies from Mesabi community college in Virginia, Minnesota. She worked as a store manager for many years while raising her two beautiful boys, Bryan and Donovan. Unfortunately, in 2021, she lost her eldest son, Bryan, unexpectedly. She loves nature, painting (anything and everything), crocheting, crafting of all kinds, photography, spending time with her family, and her newest love of writing books for young children. She currently resides on the Iron Range in Northern Minnesota with her husband, Kenny.